This library edition published in 2012 by Walter Foster Publishing, Inc.
Distributed by Black Rabbit Books.
P.O. Box 3263 Mankato, Minnesota 56002

Designed and published by Walter Foster Publishing, Inc.
Walter Foster is a registered trademark.

Printed in Mankato, Minnesota, USA by CG Book Printers, a division of Corporate Graphics.

First Library Edition

Library of Congress Cataloging-in-Publication Data

Winterberg, Jenna.
  Watch me draw a boy's adventure / story by Jenna Winterberg ;
illustrations by Diana Fisher. -- First Library Edition.
     pages cm
  ISBN 978-1-936309-79-5
  1. Drawing--Technique--Juvenile literature. 2. Drawing books--Juvenile
literature. I. Fisher, Diana, illustrator. II. Title.
  NC655.W4853 2012
  741.2--dc23
                                    2012004727

052012
17679

9 8 7 6 5 4 3 2 1

A Boy's Adventure

Story by Jenna Winterberg • Illustrations by Diana Fisher

Walter Foster

Meet Sawyer, a quiet mouse who lives a simple life out in the country, where the cows and horses graze in wide open fields, the crickets chirp well into the evening, and the scent of fresh hay and grass greets you every morning. Sawyer loves the country life because it offers so many ways to relax, such as his favorite pastime—fishing!

Draw Sawyer the mouse!

1

2

3

4

5

6

Sawyer likes fishing because it doesn't take a lot of thought—which means he can let his imagination go wild while waiting to net a fish! Today, Sawyer is daydreaming about his city cousins and how they live. He becomes so lost in thought, he doesn't notice when Simon, the snake, slithers up!

Draw Simon the snake

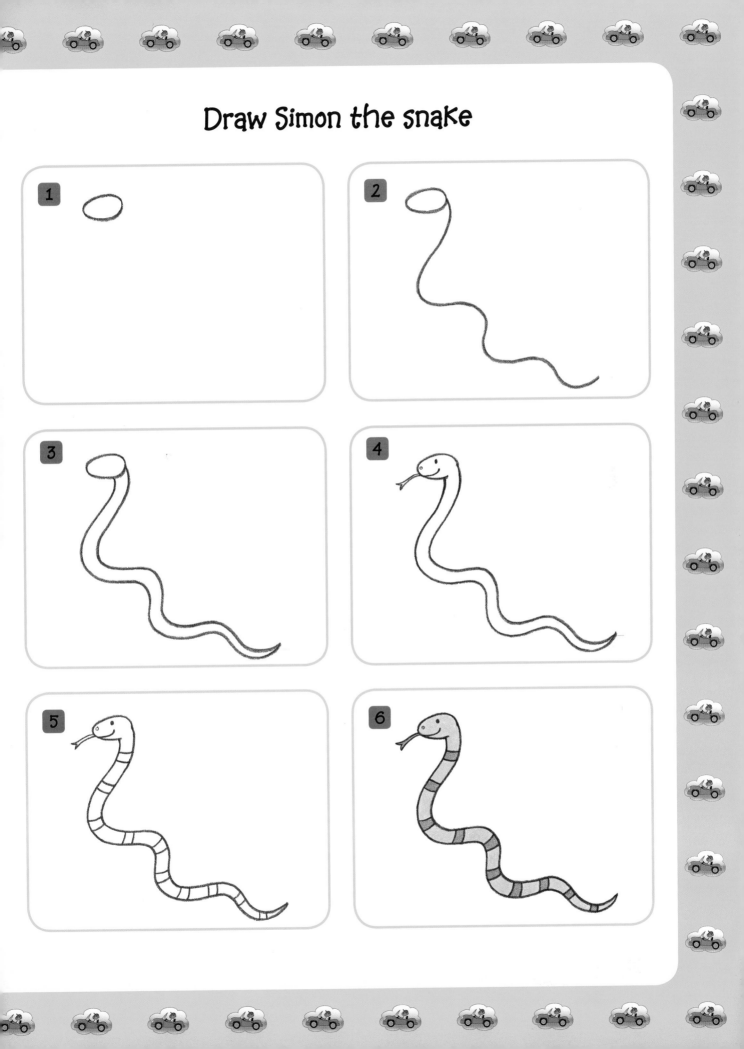

A low whisper startles Sawyer, popping his thought bubble. "Daydreaming about the sssss-city life again?" asks Simon. "Why don't you vissssssit?" Sawyer starts to respond, but Larry, the lizard, interrupts him. "I couldn't help but overhear," Larry explains, "Simon's right, you should see the city in person—not just in daydreams!"

Draw Larry the lizard!

1

2

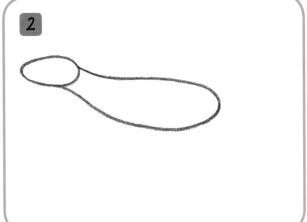

3

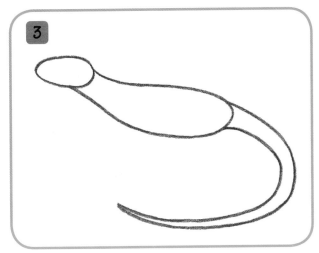

4

5

6

Sawyer gives this idea some thought. "I'd like to go to the city. And I'd really like to see my cousins! Do you think my grandpa would give me permission to go?" Simon and Larry nod in unison. "Why not asssssssk?" encourages Simon. So Sawyer gathers up his fishing gear and climbs on his skateboard, heading home to find his grandpa.

Draw the skateboard!

1

2

3

4

5

6

As the little mouse coasts toward his home, he passes his neighbor Weaver, the spider. "Hey, Sawyer!" calls out the spider, "What's the hurry?" Sawyer hollers back as he continues pushing along on his skateboard, "I'm going to ask Grandpa if I can take a trip to the city!" Weaver lets out a low whistle. "Sounds fun," he says. "Good luck!"

Draw Weaver the spider!

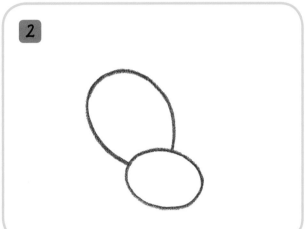

"Grandpa, Grandpa!" shouts Sawyer as he arrives at the stables where they live. "What's all this noise?" asks Grandpa, "Did you catch a trout?" Sawyer shakes his head, "No—but I caught an idea! I'd like to visit my cousins in the city." Grandpa thinks— then nods, "I have just the way to get you there." He leads Sawyer to a pickup behind the stables.

Draw the pickup truck!

1

2

3

4

5

6

Grandpa helps Sawyer up into the truck bed. Then, holding Sawyer's hand, Grandpa makes his way to the back of the truck, where another passenger waits! "Hello, Chase," says Grandpa to the friendly dog. "This is my boy, Sawyer, and I'd really appreciate it if you could keep an eye on him. He's going to visit our family in the city."

Draw Chase the dog!

1

2
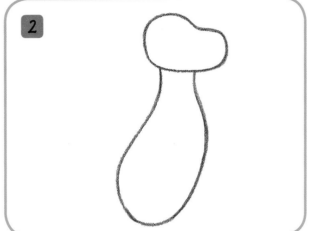

3

4

5

6

After Grandpa leaves to make arrangements for Sawyer's stay in the city, Chase nudges Sawyer. "Hey little guy," he says, "hide out in the corner for just a sec." From his hiding place, Sawyer watches as the farmer loads a glinting, gleaming motorcycle into the truck! Chase explains, "He likes to ride his bike on the smooth city streets."

Draw the motorcycle!

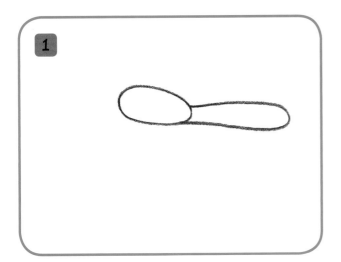

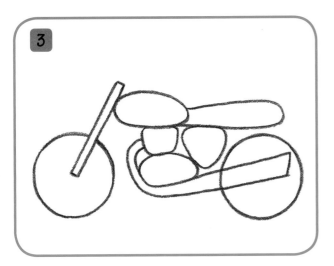

A moment later, the truck starts and they pull away. Chase entertains Sawyer with stories about the city. As the miles go by, he describes streets filled with fast cars, bright lights, and curious scents. "And you see plenty of those," Chase says, pointing to a place high in the sky. Sawyer's gaze follows—and he gets his first look at a jet plane!

Draw the jet plane!

1
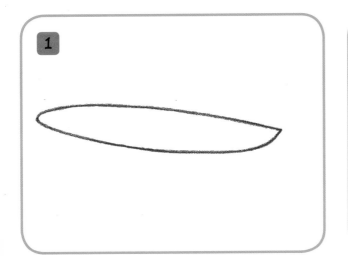

2
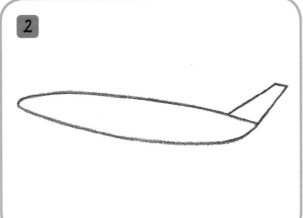

3
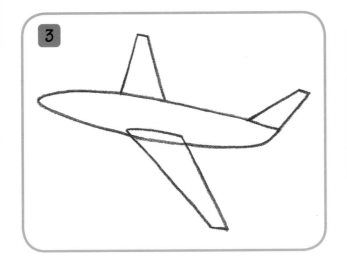

4
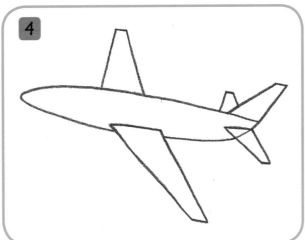

5
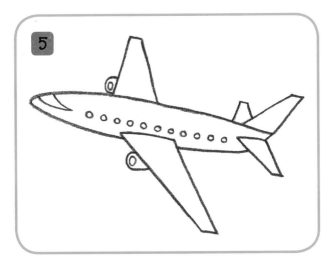

6
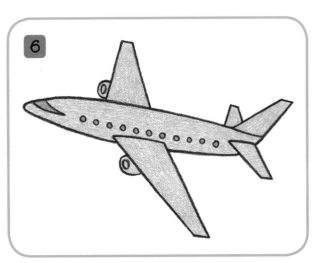

By now, Sawyer is so excited that he can hardly stand it!
He wonders aloud how much farther they have to go—
but as soon as the words are out of his mouth, he realizes
they are already there! As the truck passes a line of store
windows, Sawyer spots all sorts of TVs, computers, and
even robots—things you'd see in the city!

Draw the robot!

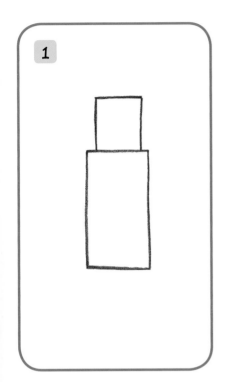

1

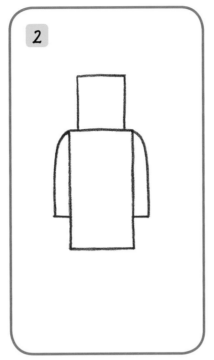

2

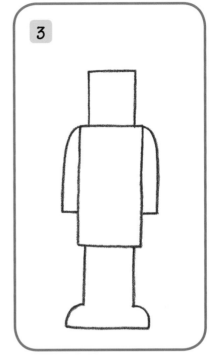

3

4

5

6

When the truck comes to a traffic light, Chase pipes up, "This is your stop, little guy!" Sawyer gulps as he cranes his neck up, up, and up, straining to see the top of the skyscraper. But he excitedly hops out of the truck as soon as he spots his cousins running toward him, waving and welcoming him to the city!

Draw the skyscraper!

The end.